Improving Reading Comprehension
Grade 2

Table of Contents

Improving Reading Comprehension
Grade 2

Introduction

Introduction

We have all watched a child struggle while learning to read. Each new word can be a challenge or a frustration. We have joined in the child's struggle, teaching the skills needed to decode unfamiliar words and make sense of the letters. Then we have experienced joy as the child mastered the words and began to read sentences, gaining confidence with each new success.

Learning to read is one of the most important skills your students will ever acquire. By the second grade, most children are well on their way to becoming confident readers. The skill that must go hand in hand with learning to read, however, is reading comprehension. When a child reads without understanding, he or she will quickly lose the joy that was discovered when each word began to make sense. Readers need to develop the skill of making sense of new words through context. They need to understand an author's message, whether stated or implied. They need to see how each event in a story affects the rest of the story and its characters. These are all important skills that must be nurtured if a student is to be a successful reader. Reading comprehension is vital throughout the curricula in school and for success in many other areas of life.

To build the necessary skills for reading comprehension, a reading program should clear away other stresses so that the student can concentrate on the reading. With that in mind, the stories in Improving Reading Comprehension have been written to interest and engage the reader. They are short to hold the reader's attention. The exercises are short but effective tools to determine the student's understanding of each story. Given as homework or class work, the two-page assignments can easily be incorporated into existing reading programs for practice and reinforcement of reading comprehension skills.

Organization

The stories in Improving Reading Comprehension have been divided into six chapters: Friends and Family, Animal Tales, Pets, Silly Stories and Fairy Tales, All About Animals, and Earth and Space. The stories are a mix of fantasy, nonfiction, and realistic fiction.

Each story includes a comprehension exercise. These exercises concentrate on the student's understanding of the story. Many exercises emphasize vocabulary as well. The exercises include completing sentences, matching words with definitions, labeling, finding words with similar meanings, multiple-choice questions, and crossword puzzles. Each story and exercise assignment is complete on two sides of one tear-out sheet.

The Curriculum Correlation chart on Page 4 will allow you to include the reading in other curriculum areas.

There is a Letter to Parents on Page 5, and a Letter to Students on Page 6.

Notifying students and parents of a new activity beforehand will help answer students' questions and keep parents informed.

There are four assessments. Each assessment can be used individually and in any order.

Use

Improving Reading Comprehension is designed for independent use by students. Copies of the stories and activities can be given to individual students, pairs of students, or small groups for completion. They can also be used as a center activity.

To begin, determine the implementation that fits your students' needs and your classroom structure. The following plan suggests a format for this implementation.

1. **Explain** the purpose of the activities to your class.

2. **Review** the mechanics of how you want students to work with the exercises. You may wish to introduce the subject of each article. You may decide to tap into students' prior knowledge of the subject for discussion. You might plan a group discussion after the reading.

3. **Remind** students that they are reading for understanding. Tell them to read carefully. Remind them to use a dictionary when necessary if the context is not enough to help them figure out a word.

4. **Determine** how you will monitor the assessments. Each assessment is designed to be used independently. You may decide to administer the assessments to the whole class, to small groups who have completed a unit, or to individuals as they work through the book. The assessments can be used as pre- and post-evaluations of the students' progress.

Additional Notes

1. **Parent Communication.** Use the Letter to Parents, and encourage the students to share the Letter to Students with their parents. Decide if you want to keep the activity pages and assessments in portfolios for conferencing, or if you want students to take them home as they are completed.

2. **Bulletin Boards.** Since a key to comprehension is discussion, encourage students to illustrate, add on to, or do further research on their favorite stories. Display the students' work on a bulletin board.

3. **Have Fun.** Reading should be fun, and the stories in Improving Reading Comprehension will capture students' interest and stimulate their imagination. Fun group discussions, ideas, or games that evolve from the reading will enhance the learning experience.

Improving Reading Comprehension
Grade 2

Curriculum Correlation

Story Title	Social Studies	Language Arts	Science	Math	PE
The Picnic		X	X		
A New Baby	X	X			
Peter and Jimmy	X	X			X
A Helping Hand	X	X			
A Good Friend		X		X	
Making Money		X		X	
Growing Up	X	X			
Jocko and Polo	X	X			
How Elephant Got His Trunk	X				
A Scare at the Top	X	X			
Ollie the Ostrich		X	X		
Sasha's Web	X	X			
How Turtle Got His Shell		X	X		
Porcupine Pals	X	X			
Penny's Puppy	X	X			
The Perfect Pet	X	X			
Darcy's Pets		X	X		
Peanut Pals		X	X		
Bunny Babies		X	X		
Tabitha's Turtle		X	X		
Dogs and More Dogs		X			
A Real Deal		X			
The Silly Sisters		X			
Jared's Wish		X			
Two Greedy Goblins		X		X	
The Foolish Farmers		X			
King Carl		X		X	
The Earthworm		X	X		
Midnight Snack		X	X		
Lucky Ducks	X	X			
Luis and the Bluebirds	X	X	X		
Whale Ways		X	X		
A Noise in the Attic		X			
The Brick Birds		X	X		
Emma's Horse		X		X	
Great Gravity		X	X		
Doug's Dream		X	X		
Islands		X	X		
Awesome Air		X	X		
The Amazing Journey	X	X			
Mighty Mountains		X	X		
The Planets		X	X		

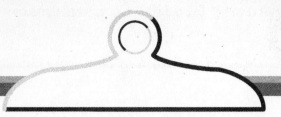

Dear Parents:

Learning to read is clearly one of the most important things your child will ever do. In second grade, most children are well on their way to becoming independent readers. They have developed a good sight vocabulary and have learned ways to decode unfamiliar words.

What is equally important for young readers, however, is reading with understanding. If your child reads a story but is unable to describe the events in his or her own words or answer questions about the story, then the reading loses its meaning. Young readers need practice to strengthen their reading comprehension abilities.

With this goal in mind, our class will be working with a book of stories and activities that will reinforce reading comprehension. The short stories are a mix of fiction and nonfiction. The stories are fun and the one-page exercises are varied. Without feeling the pressure of a long story to remember or many pages of exercises to work, your child will develop a better understanding of the reading and have fun doing it!

Occasionally, your child may bring home an activity. Please consider the following suggestions to help your child work successfully.

• Provide a quiet place to work.

• If your child is reading, help to find the meanings of difficult words through the context of the story. Discuss the story.

• Go over the directions for the exercises together.

• Check the lesson when it is complete. Note areas of improvement as well as concern.

Thank you for being involved with your child's learning. A strong reading foundation will lead to a lifetime of reading enjoyment and success.

Cordially,

Dear Student:

Do you like to read? You can probably remember your favorite story. You can probably tell a friend what happened in the story. Maybe you talked to someone in your family about it.

It is good to think and talk about what you read. This can help you remember. It can also help you to understand what you read.

We will be working with a book of short stories. After reading each one, you will have to think about the story. Then you will answer some questions. Thinking about these stories will help you practice for reading longer stories. It will help you to become a better reader.

The stories are a mix of facts and fun. There are animal adventures and stories about pets. There are silly stories and facts about Earth and space. Read carefully and have fun.
There is a story here for everyone!

Sincerely,

Assessment 1

Directions

Read the paragraph. Then choose the best word to complete each sentence. Write the word on the line.

James watched as the birds flew in and out of an arch near his front door. The arch was made of brick. It looked as if the birds were pecking at the brick. James wondered if they found insects there. The next day, James noticed that there were small mounds on the bricks. He wondered what they could be. Soon, the birds came back and began to pack grasses into the mounds. The mounds were made of mud. Over the next week, the grasses turned into a nest. Now James knew what the birds had been doing!

1. The arch was made of _____.
   a. blocks   **b.** bricks   **c.** rocks

2. James noticed small _____ on the bricks.
   a. holes   **b.** marks   **c.** mounds

3. The birds packed _____ into the mounds.
   a. grasses   **b.** glasses   **c.** seeds

4. The mounds were made of _____.
   a. sand   **b.** mud   **c.** straw

5. James saw that the birds were making a _____.
   a. rest   **b.** family   **c.** nest

Assessment 2

Directions

Read the paragraph. Choose a word from the paragraph with the same meaning as the underlined words. Write the word on the line.

The movements of the earth form mountains. The earth is made of three layers. The center of the earth is the core. It is very hot. The mantle is the next layer. It is wrapped around the core. The core heats the mantle so it is not solid. The crust covers the mantle. We live on the crust of the earth. It is made up of plates. The plates move around very slowly. When the plates move against each other, the crust folds. Mountains are formed. This rubbing can also cause earthquakes and volcanoes. A river can form mountains, too. A river can wear away land to cause a valley to form. The land around the valley becomes a mountain.

1. The <u>motions</u> of the earth form mountains. _____

2. The <u>center of the earth</u> is very hot. _____

3. We live on the <u>outer layer</u> of the earth. _____

4. The crust is made up of <u>large pieces of the earth that move</u>.

_____

5. A river wears away land to form <u>a low piece of land</u>.

_____

Assessment 3

Directions

Read the paragraphs. Then answer the questions about the story. Circle the letter in front of the correct answer.

Segi's parents were excited. Segi's mother was going to have a baby. Segi's parents spent a lot of time getting ready. They turned one room into a baby room. They got the baby crib from the attic.

Segi's friends had ideas about babies. "Babies take lots of time," said Tina. "What if your mom and dad don't have time left for you?"

"Mothers get tired with new babies," said Mimi. "They take lots of energy. Your mom won't want to play games with you." This did not sound good to Segi.

1. Why were Segi's parents excited?
   a. They found a crib in the attic.
   b. Segi's mother was going to have a baby.
   c. Segi's big sister was coming to visit.

2. Segi's friends said that babies _____.
   a. are very noisy and messy
   b. are fun to play with
   c. take lots of time and energy

3. How does Segi probably feel about the baby?
   a. worried
   b. bored
   c. happy

Name _____   Date _____

Assessment 4

Directions

Read the paragraph. Then choose a word from the paragraph that fits each clue. Write the words in the puzzle.

Len and Leona were curious. So one day they sneaked to the top of a very large tree. The sun felt warm and wonderful. They could see for miles. It was amazing! It was also very noisy. There were many birds with frightening cries. Suddenly, a bright yellow bird flew by and snatched Len from his branch. Leona screamed. Len struggled to get free. Another bird tried to grab Len. The yellow bird dropped Len. He fell down into the trees. All at once, he stopped falling. His heart was fluttering in his body. But he was safe. Then he saw Leona. "Thank goodness you are all right!" cried Leona. "Let's get home. I'll never come back here again!"

ACROSS:
1. grabbed
4. surprising

DOWN:
1. moved quietly
2. wondering about
3. not cold

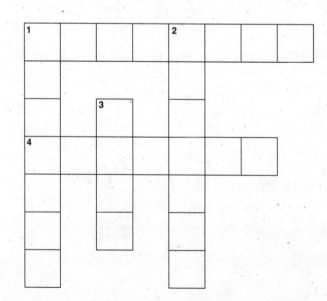

Improving Reading Comprehension 2, SV 5800-0

The Picnic

Mark and Jane are good friends. They live near each other in a little town in the mountains. One thing that both children like to do is explore new places.

One Saturday, Mark and Jane decide to explore a hill near their neighborhood. They make cheese sandwiches to take along for a picnic lunch. As they walk, the two friends talk and laugh. When they get closer to the hill, they can see a huge, gray rock near the top.

Mark calls out, "I'll race you to the rock!"

Both children run as fast as they can up the steep, grassy hill. As they reach the top, the children notice that there are large, dark clouds in the sky. Then they hear the rumble of thunder and feel a few tiny drops of cool rain.

"I think a storm is coming," says Jane.

The children run down the hill and back to Mark's house. Just as the children run inside the house, they see a bright flash of lightning and hear a loud clap of thunder. It starts to rain hard, so Mark and Jane decide to have an indoor picnic. The children sit by a large window to eat their sandwiches and watch the storm.

Go on to next page.

Directions

Answer each question about the story. Circle the letter in front of the correct answer.

1. Where do Mark and Jane live?
   a. near a park   **c.** in the woods
   b. in the mountains   **d.** in the city

2. What do they make for their picnic lunch?
   a. ham sandwiches   **c.** carrot sticks
   b. pasta salad   **d.** cheese sandwiches

3. What do they see at the top of the hill?
   a. a huge rock   **c.** a pretty meadow
   b. an old castle   **d.** a strange man

4. How do the children know it is going to rain?
   a. They hear the weather report.
   b. Their parents tell them.
   c. They see clouds and hear thunder.
   d. It always rains when they have a picnic.

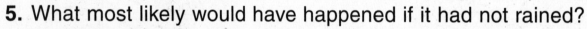

5. What most likely would have happened if it had not rained?
   a. It would have snowed instead.
   b. Mark and Jane would have had their picnic outside.
   c. Their parents would have made them come home.
   d. Mark and Jane would have had their picnic inside anyway.

A New Baby

Segi's parents were very happy. Segi's mother was going to have a baby. Segi's father said Segi would love being a big sister. Segi was not so sure.

Segi's parents were excited. They spent a lot of time getting ready. They turned one room into a baby room. They got the baby crib from the attic. Segi's friends had ideas about babies. "Babies take lots of time," said Tina. "What if your mom and dad don't have time left for you?"

"Mothers get tired with new babies," said Mimi. "They take lots of energy. Your mom won't want to play games with you." This did not sound good to Segi.

Segi watched her mother's stomach. It got bigger and bigger. Soon the baby would arrive. One night, Segi began to cry. She told her mother what her friends had said. Segi didn't want a new baby. Her mother held her. "Segi," she said, "you will always be very special. It won't matter how many babies we have."

Segi's mother went to the hospital. Two days later, she brought home a baby boy. Segi thought he was a beautiful baby. Her father lifted her up for a better look. Segi said, "Hi, little brother. I'm your big sister, Segi!"

Go on to next page.

Name_____ Date_____

Directions

Choose the word that best fits each sentence. Write the word in the blank.

1. Segi's parents were _____.
   mean   excited   elves

2. Segi's mother was going to have a _____.
   baby   band   busy

3. Segi's father said she would like being a big _____.
   sitter   brother   sister

4. Tina said that babies take lots of _____.
   tickle   time   worry

5. Mimi said that Segi's mom would not want to play

   _____ with her.
   games   garage   tag

6. Segi watched her mother's _____ grow bigger.
   eyes   stomach   sneaker

7. Her mother told Segi that she would always be _____.
   sharp   favorite   special

8. Segi thought her baby brother was _____.
   broken   beautiful   behind

Peter and Jimmy

Peter likes his big brother, Jimmy. Peter always waits for Jimmy to come home from school in the afternoon. He waves to Jimmy from the window, and this makes Jimmy smile. Peter always asks his big brother to play with him. Most of the time, Jimmy plays with his friends from school. Peter wishes that his big brother would play with him, too.

One day, Jimmy comes home from school and says, "Come on, Peter, let's go outside and play ball." Peter is so excited! They race to see who can get to the tree in the yard first. Jimmy wins.

Then Jimmy throws the ball to Peter. Peter tries to throw the ball back to Jimmy, but the ball rolls on the ground part of the way. Then Jimmy shows Peter how to kick the ball across the yard. Peter likes this game because he can kick the ball almost as far as Jimmy can. They are having fun taking turns kicking the ball. Jimmy shows Peter how to kick the ball high in the air. The two brothers play together until it is time for Jimmy to do his homework.

Go on to next page.

Name_____   Date_____

Answer each question about the story. Circle the letter in front of the correct answer.

1. Who is Jimmy?

    a. Peter's cousin   **c.** Peter's father

    b. Peter's little brother   **d.** Peter's older brother

2. Jimmy plays with _____ most of the time.

    a. his brother, Peter   **c.** Peter's friends

    b. his school friends   **d.** his sister

3. What is Peter's favorite game?

    a. kicking the ball

    b. batting the ball

    c. throwing the ball

    d. bouncing the ball

4. Why do the brothers stop playing?

    a. Peter has to do his chores.

    b. Jimmy has to do his homework.

    c. Their mother calls them inside.

    d. They are too tired to keep playing.

5. Why does Peter probably like to play with Jimmy?

    a. Peter can win all the games they play together.

    b. Peter doesn't have any friends to play with.

    c. Peter looks up to Jimmy because he is his older brother.

    d. Jimmy lets Peter win sometimes.

A Helping Hand

Robert watched his grandfather. He was moving boxes and tools around in the garage. Then he began to sweep the dirt from the garage floor. Robert was getting impatient. He had already waited while his grandfather put away some groceries. His grandfather had told him that they could go fishing today. It would be their first fishing trip this year.

Robert could hardly wait to go. He could imagine how it would feel to cast his line into the water. He thought about how it felt when a fish took the bait. His line would tighten. The pole would bend a little. Then Robert would reel in the big one! But first, he had to wait for his grandfather. He had a lot of work to do.

Suddenly, Robert had an idea. He went to his grandfather and took the broom. He began to do the sweeping himself. His grandfather went back to moving the boxes. They finished cleaning the garage in no time. Then Robert got a bucket full of soapy water. He and his grandfather soaped up the truck. Then Robert hosed off all the soap. The truck sparkled in the sunshine.

"Well, Robert!" said his grandfather. "With you helping me, my work went much faster! Now we have just one more thing to do."

Robert sighed. "What now?" he thought. "We will never go fishing!"

"We have to get our fishing poles and get going!" said his grandfather, laughing.

Go on to next page.

Name _____ Date _____

Directions

Read each clue. Choose a word from the Word List that fits each clue. Write the words in the puzzle.

Word List

cast imagine groceries bait
sparkled garage impatient reel

ACROSS:

3. shined

4. food from the store

7. used to catch fish

8. not wanting to wait

DOWN:

1. pull in

2. place to put car

5. throw out

6. make up in your mind

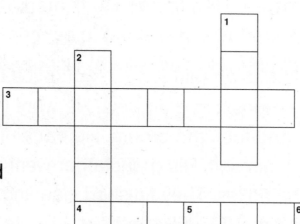

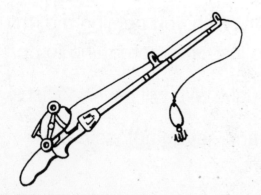

A Good Friend

Margaret was sad because she could not go out to play. She watched her two brothers and their friends play outside. Margaret had broken her arm yesterday and she was sad.

"Margaret, why don't you read a book?" her father asked.

"No, I don't feel like it." Margaret just sat and looked out the window. She played with her cat for a little while.

When the doorbell rang, Margaret thought that one of her brother's friends had come by. But instead it was her friend Kim from school.

"Hello, Margaret," said Kim. "I heard you broke your arm."

"Yes, and I can't go outside to play," Margaret told her.

"Why don't we play in here?" Kim asked. "We could play a game or color some pictures." Margaret liked Kim's idea, and they played a game on the floor.

"I like playing this game with you," Margaret said. "Can you come to my house again tomorrow?"

Go on to next page.

Directions

Answer each question about the story. Circle the letter in front of the correct answer.

1. Why does Margaret stay inside?
   a. Her brothers are playing.
   b. She has broken her arm.
   c. She is reading a book.
   d. She is happy.

2. Who is Margaret's friend from school?
   a. Jennifer
   b. Michelle
   c. Kim
   d. Monica

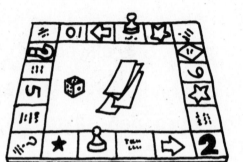

3. Why does Margaret's friend come to visit?
   a. to play
   b. to eat
   c. to sleep
   d. to work

4. Why does Margaret ask her friend to visit the next day?
   a. She likes the cat.
   b. She wants to go outside.
   c. She does not feel like it.
   d. She likes Kim.

5. What do you think the two friends will play the next day?
   a. kickball   **b.** checkers
   c. tag   **d.** hide-and-seek

Making Money

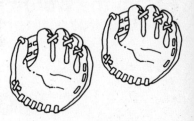

Gordon and Daniel looked at the baseball gloves on the store shelf. The glove Gordon wanted was $13.95, and Daniel's was $15.95. Now they had to think of a way to earn the money to buy the gloves.

The first idea that the boys had was to help with spring cleanup. They got rakes and big garbage bags. They asked their neighbors if they could rake up the old leaves from last fall. They raked Mr. Small's yard. It was hard work. He had many trees! When the work was complete, he paid them each $5.00.

"Thanks, Mr. Small!" said the boys.

They collected $3.00 each from Mrs. Hertz, and $2.00 each from Mrs. Perez. Now all Gordon needed was $3.95. Daniel needed $5.95 more.

"How can we earn some more money?" asked Gordon. "Do you have anything you could sell?"

"I have some old toys," said Daniel. "Go get some of yours and meet me in my driveway. I'll set up a table."

The boys ran to their houses. They searched for toys they did not use anymore. They piled them on a table in Daniel's driveway. They put out a sign. It said, "Toys—Make an Offer!" Children from the neighborhood gathered around the table. Soon, all the toys were gone. The boys counted the money. There was more than enough!

Gordon and Daniel rode their bikes to the store. The gloves were still there. They bought an ice cream on the way home with the extra money. They needed energy for their first practice that night!

Go on to next page.

Directions

Rewrite each sentence. Use a word with the same meaning from the Word List in place of the underlined words.

Word List

extra garbage earn neighbors
collected energy searched completed

1. The boys got <u>trash</u> bags to fill with leaves. _____

_____

2. They did cleanup work for <u>the people who lived nearby.</u> _____

_____

3. The boys <u>finished</u> the work in Mr. Small's yard. _____

_____

4. Gordon and Daniel <u>were given</u> money for their work. _____

_____

5. The boys needed to <u>make</u> enough to buy gloves. _____

_____

6. They <u>looked</u> for toys they did not use. _____

_____

7. Gordon and Daniel had <u>leftover</u> money for ice cream. _____

_____

8. They needed <u>power</u> for their first practice. _____

_____

Name _____   Date _____

Growing Up

Terry is five years old. He thinks he is old enough to walk to the school bus stop by himself. But his mother is not so sure.

"Wait until you are six, Terry," she says. "Then you will be old enough to cross the street by yourself."

"I can do it, Mom," says Terry. "I have watched the older children cross the street." She tells him to wait until he is older.

Every day Terry's mother walks with him to the corner. She and Terry talk about how to cross the street to get to the bus stop. Terry listens and tries to remember the safety rules. Every morning Terry asks his mother whether he can walk to the bus stop by himself. One morning, his mother says, "Yes."

Terry leaves the house and skips down the sidewalk. He is so happy! When he gets to the corner, he looks both ways and crosses the street when there are no cars coming. On the other side of the street, Terry looks back and sees his mother on the front porch of their house. Terry smiles and waves to her. She smiles and waves back. This makes Terry feel warm and happy. He cannot wait to get to school!

Go on to next page.

Name_____ Date_____

Directions

Answer each question about the story. Circle the letter in front of the correct answer.

1. What does Terry want to do?

   a. stay in the house
   b. walk to the bus stop alone
   c. wave to his mother
   d. skip down the sidewalk

2. What does Terry need to learn?
   a. how to cross the street safely
   b. how to read
   c. how to find the bus stop
   d. how to sing a new song

3. When Terry walks to the bus stop alone, his mother _____.
   a. stays at the house
   b. follows in the car
   c. walks behind him
   d. gets on the bus

4. What does Terry do by himself?
   a. He walks to school.
   b. He reads a book.
   c. He walks to the bus stop.
   d. He uses the telephone.

5. How does Terry feel as he leaves the house alone?
   a. scared   **c.** sad
   b. lost   **d.** proud

Jocko and Polo

Jocko, the lion, was the ruler of the jungle. He was mean and he liked to scare the other animals. When Jocko was near, the other animals ran away. Jocko did not have any friends.

One day, some hunters caught Jocko with a net. They put him in a cage and carried him off to their village. Luckily, Polo, one of the other lions, saw what happened. He asked the other animals to help save Jocko, but they did not want to help. They were glad that Jocko was gone. So that night, Polo went alone to try to save Jocko.

Jocko was surprised when he saw Polo. "Why have you come to help me, Polo?" asked Jocko. "I have never been nice to you."

"I know, Jocko. But animals must stick together against the hunters." Polo unlocked the cage and set Jocko free. Then they left the village and crawled safely back into the jungle.

When the other animals saw Jocko, they began to run.

"No! Stop!" roared Jocko. "Do not be afraid of me. I have learned my lesson. I have my friend, Polo, to thank for that." From then on, Jocko and the other animals lived in peace.

Go on to next page.

Directions

Answer each question about the story. Circle the letter in front of the correct answer.

1. Why doesn't Jocko have any friends?
  a. He does not want any.   **c.** Jocko scares the other animals.
  b. He lives alone.   **d.** Hunters capture him.

2. How do the hunters capture Jocko?
  a. They chase him into a pit.
  b. They catch him with a net.
  c. Polo tricks Jocko.
  d. The animals trap him.

3. The animals do not want to save Jocko because they _____.
  a. are tired of being frightened by him
  b. do not think they can get him out of the cage
  c. are afraid of the hunters
  d. do not know where he is

4. Jocko is surprised to see Polo because _____.
  a. Polo scares Jocko
  b. Jocko thinks no one knows where he is
  c. the hunters captured Polo, too
  d. Jocko knows none of the animals likes him

5. After Polo saves Jocko, they _____.
  a. become friends
  b. scare the other animals
  c. scare the hunters
  d. leave the jungle

How Elephant Got His Trunk

One day long ago, Elephant came to a pond to drink the cool water. He saw Crocodile taking a nap. Elephant and Crocodile often liked to tease each other. So, Elephant decided to play a trick on Crocodile.

While Crocodile was sleeping, Elephant put some mud into Crocodile's ears. Elephant thought to himself how surprised Crocodile would be when he woke up and could not hear.

After a while, Elephant woke Crocodile. Crocodile said, "How are you today, Elephant?" Elephant seemed only to move his mouth as if he were speaking. Now, Crocodile was clever, and he realized what Elephant had done. So he decided to play his own trick on Elephant.

Crocodile said, "I can't hear you. Please come a little closer."

When Elephant got close enough, Crocodile snapped with his jaws and grabbed Elephant's tiny nose. Elephant pulled and pulled to try to get away. The more Elephant pulled, the more his nose stretched.

In the end, Elephant pulled free, but not before his nose had stretched into a long trunk. That is why, to this day, elephants have long trunks.

Go on to next page.

Directions

Answer each question about the story. Circle the letter in front of the correct answer.

1. What kind of nose did Elephant have long ago?
   a. long
   c. small
   b. large
   d. pointy

2. How does Elephant trick Crocodile?
   a. He splashes Crocodile with water.
   b. He snaps at Crocodile's nose.
   c. He pulls Crocodile's tail.
   d. He puts mud in Crocodile's ears.

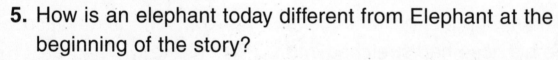

3. How does Crocodile trick Elephant?
   a. He tells Elephant a joke.
   b. He pulls Elephant's tail.
   c. He grabs Elephant's nose.
   d. He puts mud in Elephant's nose.

4. How does Elephant's nose change?
   a. It gets longer.
   c. It gets fatter.
   b. It gets smaller.
   d. It gets wider.

5. How is an elephant today different from Elephant at the beginning of the story?
   a. It has a trunk.
   c. It is clever.
   b. It has strong legs.
   d. It has large ears.

A Scare at the Top

Len Lizard lived deep in the forest. His best friend was Leona Lizard. Len and Leona played together in the leafy growth. They looked for bugs in the bark and under the leaves. They loved to feel the sunlight when it peeked in.

Len and Leona were curious. They wanted to see the canopy. It was high up in the forest. They had heard about its bright sunshine and the wonderful things to see. But it was no place for little lizards, their mothers said. Too many birds would love to snack on little Len and Leona!

Still, they were curious. So one day they sneaked to the top of a very large tree. The sun felt warm and wonderful. They could see for miles. It was amazing! It was also very noisy. There were many birds with frightening cries. Suddenly, a bright yellow bird flew by and snatched Len from his branch. Leona screamed. Len struggled to get free. The yellow bird dropped Len. He fell down into the trees. His heart was fluttering in his body. But he was safe. Then he saw Leona. "Thank goodness you are all right!" cried Leona. "Let's get home. I'll never come back here again!"

"Yes," answered Len, "our mothers were right. This is no place for us!" They crawled quickly back down the tree. Len's body was sore where the bird's beak had held him. They reached home safely. "Maybe," said Len, "we can go back again when we're older. We're already wiser!"

Go on to next page.

Name_____ Date_____

Directions

Read each clue. Choose a word from the Word List that fits each clue. Write the words in the puzzle.

Word List

leap fluttering growth sore
amazing canopy snatched curious

ACROSS:

1. high up in the forest
3. surprising
5. trembling
7. leaves and branches

DOWN:

1. wondering about
2. jump
4. grabbed
6. hurting

Improving Reading Comprehension 2, SV 5800-0

Ollie the Ostrich

All the birds were very proud that they could fly. All the birds, that is, except Ollie. Ollie was an ostrich. She could not fly. She was not tiny like the other birds. Instead, she was large and fluffy and had long, strong legs. Ollie did not like being different from the other birds. Most of all, she wished that she could fly.

One day there was a terrible fire. Ollie and the other birds had to flee for their lives. As the fire grew, the smoke became so thick that the birds in the sky dropped to the ground. All, that is, except Ollie. She was already on the ground.

When she saw that the other birds were in trouble, she picked them up and put them on her big, fluffy back. Then she ran as fast as she could with her long, strong legs. She carried the other birds to safety.

Afterwards, one of the little birds said to Ollie, "Thank you, Ollie. I wish I had long, strong legs like you." Ollie thought about that for a moment, and then she smiled a great big ostrich smile.

Go on to next page.

Directions

Answer each question about the story. Circle the letter in front of the correct answer.

1. How is Ollie different from the other birds?

   a. She has feathers.   **c.** She gets away from the fire.

   b. She is fast.   **d.** She cannot fly.

2. How does Ollie feel at the beginning of the story?

   a. happy   **c.** proud

   b. sad   **d.** excited

3. What terrible thing happens?

   a. The other birds fly away.

   b. There is a fire.

   c. Ollie hurts her leg.

   d. Ollie runs away from the fire.

4. How does Ollie help the other birds?

   a. She saves them from the fire.

   b. She teaches them to fly.

   c. She races with the other birds.

   d. She plays with the other birds.

5. What makes Ollie happy?

   a. She likes her long, strong legs.

   b. She learns to fly.

   c. She is like the other birds.

   d. She plays with the other ostriches.

Sasha's Web

Sasha watched as the other spiders crawled up the walls of the barn. They spun beautiful webs in the corners by the ceiling. She wished she could spin a beautiful web high up in a corner. But Sasha was afraid of high places. Every time she tried to climb, she got dizzy and fell.

One day, Sasha was spinning her web on the ground beside the farmer's tool bench. The farmer's son came into the barn. He ran over to where Sasha was and began to look through the tools. All of a sudden, a foot came down right beside her. The boy was in a big hurry. He was not watching where he was stepping.

Sasha had to do something. So she closed her eyes and crawled up the wall. When she opened her eyes, she found herself high above the ground. She almost fell from fright! Since the boy was still down below, she spun a web in the corner and waited.

The other spiders came over to her and admired her web. Soon, Sasha forgot about being afraid. After that, Sasha always found the highest place in the barn to spin her web.

Go on to next page.

Directions _____

Answer each question about the story. Circle the letter in front of the correct answer.

1. What does Sasha wish for?
   a. for the boy to see her   **c.** to spin a web up high
   b. a beautiful web   **d.** for the other spiders to help her

2. Why can't Sasha spin webs in high places?
   a. The other spiders push her away.
   b. She is afraid of heights.
   c. The farm boy almost steps on her.
   d. Her webs are ugly.

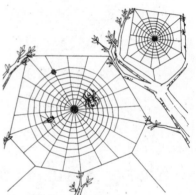

3. Sasha crawls up the wall to _____.
   a. talk to the other spiders
   b. jump on the boy
   c. spin a web
   d. get away from the boy

4. When Sasha is in the corner, the other spiders _____.
   a. come to look at her web
   b. jump on the boy
   c. crawl down the wall
   d. fall from the corners

5. Why does Sasha spin her webs in high places now?
   a. She likes to look at the sky.
   b. She is afraid the boy will bother her again.
   c. She is not afraid of high places anymore.
   d. She is afraid of spiders.

How Turtle Got His Shell

One day Turtle decided to go for a long walk to the shore. He wanted to see the ocean. When he started out, the sun was shining. It felt nice on his back. But after a while, the sky got cloudy. A rain shower fell. Turtle got all wet. He didn't feel very good. Then the sun came back out, and a gentle breeze dried Turtle.

Turtle stopped for lunch under a big oak tree. While he was eating, an acorn fell from the tree. Turtle tried to get out of the way, but the nut hit him on the head. "Ouch!" said Turtle.

Soon he arrived at the beach. He was thrilled to see the great waves. The sand felt warm and soft under his feet. Then he saw something awful. A seagull was attacking a crab! The bird swooped down and pecked at the crab. Then Turtle noticed that a hard shell protected Crab. Crab was able to get away without being hurt by the bird. Suddenly, the bird saw Turtle. What would he do? He began to hurry along the beach. Just ahead of him, he saw an old clam shell. He scurried under it for protection. He heard the seagull's beak hit the shell. Then he heard the bird's angry cry as it flew away. "That was close," thought Turtle. "I'd better keep this shell to be safe."

Turtle discovered that he liked having a shell. He could not move as quickly, but he could hide from the rain and the hot sun. When acorns fell from the trees, he would not be hurt. To this day, all the turtles you see will have a shell.

Go on to next page.

Name_____   Date_____

Directions

Choose a word from the Word List that has the same meaning as the underlined word. Write your choice on the line.

Word List

found   beach   excited   terrible
soft   flew   safety   hurried

1. Turtle went for a walk to the <u>shore</u>. _____

2. A <u>gentle</u> breeze dried Turtle. _____

3. Turtle was <u>thrilled</u> to see the waves. _____

4. Then he saw something <u>awful</u>. _____

5. The bird <u>swooped</u> down on the crab. _____

6. Turtle <u>scurried</u> under a clam shell. _____

7. Turtle used the shell for <u>protection</u>. _____

8. Turtle <u>discovered</u> that he liked the shell. _____

Porcupine Pals

Priscilla and Susan are friends. Not too long ago, these porcupines did not like each other at all. Priscilla likes to play with friends. She asked Susan to play. Susan looked up from the book she was reading and said, "Priscilla, I do not want to play."

"Why not? You can't read books and stay in the house all the time," Priscilla said. The two of them began to argue. They argued over who was smarter and who had more quills on her back. They argued about everything.

One day Priscilla was upset. She had to study for a spelling test, and she was worried. Susan felt sorry for her and said, "I'll help you study, Priscilla. We will work together, and you will do well on the test."

The two porcupines worked together, and the next day Priscilla spelled every word correctly on the test.

Ever since then, they have been best friends. Susan and Priscilla read books together and go outside to play.

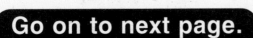

Go on to next page.

Name_____ Date_____

Directions

Answer each question about the story. Circle the letter in front of the correct answer.

1. What does Priscilla like to do?
   a. listen to music
   b. play with friends
   c. read books
   d. wash clothes

2. What does Susan like to do?
   a. talk on the telephone
   b. cook dinner
   c. draw
   d. read books

3. Why do Susan and Priscilla argue?
   a. They like to do different things.
   b. They like to things together.
   c. They like to do the same things.
   d. They like to go out.

4. How does Priscilla feel when she does well on her spelling test?
   a. angry   **c.** happy
   b. sleepy   **d.** hungry

5. Why do Priscilla and Susan become good friends?
   a. They do not like each other.
   b. They like each other.
   c. They talk on the telephone.
   d. They stay at home all the time.

Penny's Puppy

Penny hated to get up in the morning. Every morning at seven o'clock, her mother would call, "Penny! Time to get up!" Penny would just go back to sleep.

"I hate to get up in the morning!" Penny said to herself.

One day, Penny's mother and father brought home a puppy. Penny was very happy and told her parents, "I will take good care of him."

Penny named the little dog Brownie. Brownie slept on a blanket in Penny's room. The next morning, Brownie jumped onto Penny's bed and licked her face. Penny laughed. "Do you want to go for a walk?" she asked.

Penny took the dog to the backyard. He ran and played as Penny watched. When she went back into the house, her mother was awake. "Penny," she said, "it is six o'clock in the morning! Why are you up so early today?"

"Brownie wanted to go for a walk," Penny told her mother.

"I thought you didn't like to get up early in the morning," Penny's mother said.

"Now I do," laughed Penny. "I have to take care of Brownie."

Go on to next page.

Directions

Answer each question about the story. Circle the letter in front of the correct answer.

1. Why does Penny hate to get up in the morning?

    a. She likes to go swimming.   **c.** She does not like to sleep.

    b. She likes to sleep.   **d.** She likes to wake up.

2. What is the name of Penny's dog?

    a. Mother   **c.** Rusty

    b. Father   **d.** Brownie

3. Why does Penny's dog wake her up?

    a. The dog is sleepy.

    b. The dog is angry.

    c. The dog wants to go outside.

    d. The dog is hungry.

4. How does Penny feel about getting up for her dog?

    a. happy

    b. mad

    c. tired

    d. upset

5. Why does Penny want to take care of her dog?

    a. She loves school.

    b. She loves the morning.

    c. She loves to walk.

    d. She loves her dog.

The Perfect Pet

Jordan wanted a pet. He had been asking his parents for a pet for weeks. Jordan kept thinking of pets that he thought would be good. But his mother or father always had a reason why his idea was not a good one.

Jordan had asked his mother for a dog. He promised to take good care of it. He would take it for a walk every day. But his mother said that the dog might bark while they were gone. And a dog needed space. Their apartment was very small.

Then Jordan asked for a cat. But his father was allergic to cats. If he got near a cat, he would begin to sneeze and his eyes would water.

Jordan asked about a snake. He thought a snake would be quiet. A snake would not take up much room. Jordan's father was not allergic to snakes. But his mother said she could not live with a snake!

Jordan walked home from school sadly. He thought, "I will never get a pet." He stopped on the wooden bridge and looked into the water. Suddenly he had another idea. He ran all the way to his apartment. He burst through the door.

"I have thought of the perfect pet!" said Jordan to his mother. "I will get fish! Fish are quiet. They live in a small tank. They won't make Dad sneeze. And they won't bother you! What do you think?"

"I think you are right, Jordan," said his mother, smiling. "I think you have thought of the perfect pet!"

Go on to next page.

Name _____   Date _____

Directions

Choose the word that best fits each sentence. Write the word in the blank.

1. Jordan wanted a _____.

   pest   pet   pen

2. His mother said a dog needed _____.

   space   friends   lace

3. A cat would make Jordan's father _____.

   happy   hairy   sneeze

4. His mother could not _____ with a snake.

   life   dance   live

5. A fish would be a _____ pet.

   quiet   quite   quick

6. Fish live in a _____.

   trunk   table   tank

Draw a picture of the perfect pet for you.

Darcy's Pets

Darcy has many pets. She has two dogs, five cats, and three rabbits. Every time Darcy finds an animal that is hurt or lost, she takes it home with her. Darcy tries to find the lost animals' owners. If she cannot find the owners, Darcy's parents let her keep the animals as long as she takes care of them.

Darcy always has a busy day taking care of her pets. She feeds all her animals. She gives them fresh water to drink. The animals need to exercise, so Darcy lets them take turns running and playing in the backyard. Sometimes she brushes her animals or gives one of them a bath. Even with all this work, Darcy finds time to hold and pet her animals. This is the job she likes best of all.

Darcy works hard to take care of her pets. She learns a lot about dogs, cats, and rabbits. She hopes to be a veterinarian someday so she can take care of more animals.

Go on to next page.

Directions

Answer each question about the story. Circle the letter in front of the correct answer.

1. What does Darcy have in her backyard?

   a. a swing set   **c.** friends

   b. newspapers   **d.** pets

2. Why does Darcy have so many pets?

   a. She buys the pets at the pet store.

   b. She finds animals that have no homes.

   c. Darcy's friends give their pets to her.

   d. The veterinarian gives the pets to Darcy.

3. How does Darcy take care of her pets?

   a. She gives the pets to her friends.

   b. She asks her parents to take care of the pets.

   c. She feeds her pets and lets them exercise.

   d. She gives toys to her pets.

4. What is Darcy's favorite way to take care of her animals?

   a. feed them

   b. pet them

   c. walk them

   d. brush them

5. Why does Darcy want to become a veterinarian?

   a. She likes to take care of animals.

   b. She needs a job.

   c. She does not like animals.

   d. She wants to learn about plants.

Peanut Pals

Maya held the peanut out to the little chipmunk. He scampered right over to her and took it. He put it into the pouch in his cheek along with the others.

Maya had seen the chipmunk on one of her first visits to the park. She always brought nuts with her and each time she offered them to the chipmunk, he came closer and closer. Now he was not at all afraid to take the treats that Maya brought. Maya named him Chip, and she loved to visit him.

One day Maya decided to bring Chip home. Then she could see him all the time. He would be her pet. She bought a roomy cage and put soft wood curls on the bottom. She put in a little house. She put some nuts in the cage. Chip went to investigate the nuts in the cage. Maya closed the door and carried Chip home.

Soon Maya could see that Chip was not happy in his cage. She realized that Chip needed to be back in the park where he had a lot of room to play. Maya felt very sorry for taking Chip from his home. The next day, she carried the cage back to the park and set Chip free. He ran away quickly, and Maya thought she might never see him again. Still, she knew she had done the right thing.

Maya went back to the park a week later. She brought some nuts, but she did not expect to see Chip. He was probably afraid of her now, she thought. She sat on a bench and set out the peanuts. She began to read. Suddenly, she saw something moving. She turned to see her old friend Chip stuffing his face with the peanuts, just like always!

Go on to next page.

Directions

Read each clue. Choose a word from the Word List that fits each clue. Write the words in the puzzle.

Word List

offered   scampered   pouch   realized
expect   free   roomy   investigate

ACROSS:
1. knew
4. think will happen
6. in the wild
7. gave

DOWN:
1. large
2. look into
3. ran
5. sack

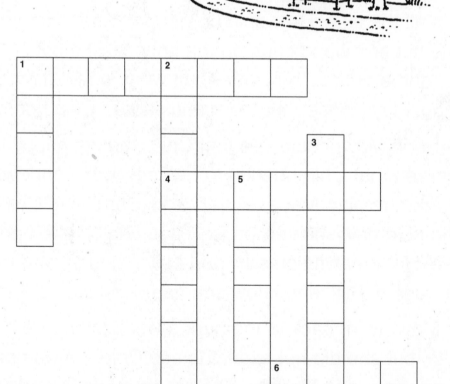

Bunny Babies

Mrs. Kelp wanted a pet to keep her company. She went to the pet store to look at the kittens and puppies. But when she got there, she saw a fat, fluffy, white rabbit. Mrs. Kelp decided she would buy the rabbit.

When she got home she made a little bed for the rabbit, which she named Snowball. She played with Snowball and watched her hop around the house. Mrs. Kelp was very happy. A fluffy rabbit was the perfect pet.

One morning Mrs. Kelp went over to Snowball's little bed and found five baby rabbits nestled up to Snowball. Soon the baby rabbits grew up. Mrs. Kelp decided to give away some of the rabbits. She took the rabbits to the school near her house. She gave the rabbits to the teachers and the children. Everyone was very happy, and they thanked Mrs. Kelp very much for her gift.

When Mrs. Kelp went home, there were only two rabbits left. Snowball and one of her grown-up babies, named Snowshoe, were sound asleep in their little bed.

Go on to next page.

Directions

Answer each question about the story. Circle the letter in front of the correct answer.

1. What does Mrs. Kelp buy at the pet store?
   a. a puppy   **c.** a rabbit
   b. a kitten   **d.** five rabbits

2. Why is Mrs. Kelp happy with Snowball?
   a. The rabbit sits by the window.
   b. Snowball is a good pet.
   c. The children at school take care of the rabbit.
   d. Snowball does tricks for her.

3. What does Mrs. Kelp do with some of the rabbits?
   a. takes them back to the pet store
   b. makes beds for them
   c. lets them play in the yard
   d. gives them to the children at school

4. How many rabbits does Mrs. Kelp give away?
   a. two
   b. six
   c. four
   d. one

5. Why does Mrs. Kelp decide to give some of the rabbits away?
   a. She has too many rabbits.
   b. She does not like rabbits.
   c. The rabbits make too much noise.
   d. She wants to make the rabbits happy.

Tabitha's Turtle

Tabitha has a turtle for a pet. She has named her pet turtle Tyrone. He lives in an aquarium in Tabitha's bedroom.

Tyrone is a box turtle. His shell is a pattern of black and yellow. When Tyrone is frightened, he pulls his head and feet into his shell. Sometimes he does this when Tabitha wants to show him to a friend. No matter what she says, he will not come out. So Tabitha sets Tyrone in his aquarium. Then she and her friend stay very quiet. They wait for timid Tyrone to peer out of his shell. Soon he knows there is no danger. He comes out and begins to move around again!

Tyrone likes to eat grass. For treats, Tabitha brings him worms and bugs. Sometimes she brings him fruit to eat. He loves fruit. Tyrone loves to eat. Tabitha has to be careful that she does not feed him too much.

Tabitha takes Tyrone outside when the weather is nice. She lets him walk around in the backyard. He eats the grass. Tabitha loves her little box turtle.

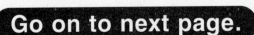

Go on to next page.

Name_____   Date_____

Choose a word from the Word List to match each meaning.
Write the word on the line.

Word List

aquarium   pattern   danger   box turtle
timid   peer   treats   frightened

1. to look out _____

2. the same shapes used over and over _____

3. something that is not safe _____

4. afraid _____

5. a glass box for a pet _____

6. shy _____

7. tasty snacks _____

8. a reptile with a shell _____

Dogs and More Dogs

Once upon a time there was a nice old man and a nice old woman. They lived in a very pretty house that had flowers growing all around it. The old woman spent her time picking the flowers and putting them in every room in the house. Their house was always filled with beautiful flowers.

Something was wrong, though. The old man and the old woman were lonely. One day the old woman said to the old man, "I like taking care of my flowers, but I wish we had a dog."

So the man left his house and went to look for a dog. He walked by a farm. He saw a cow and a horse, but he did not see a dog. He walked into the forest. He saw a fox and a deer, but he did not see a dog. As he came out of the forest, he heard a funny sound. He looked across a field, and he knew what the sound was. It was the barking of dogs. The field was full of dogs! There were hundreds of dogs!

"I choose this dog," said the old man. Then he saw another dog that was so cute he could not bear to leave it behind. Before he knew it, he had chosen them all.

Go on to next page.

Directions

Answer each question about the story. Circle the letter in front of the correct answer.

1. What does the old woman do?

   a. picks flowers   **c.** cleans the house

   b. waters the grass   **d.** reads the newspaper

2. What is wrong?

   a. The old man and old woman are lonely.

   b. The old man and old woman are hungry.

   c. The old woman does not like flowers.

   d. The old woman is lost.

3. What does the old woman want?

   a. a cat

   b. a dog

   c. a horse

   d. a pig

4. Why does the old man go to get a dog?

   a. He does not like cats.

   b. He wants to make the old woman happy.

   c. He wants to go for a walk.

   d. He does not like flowers.

5. Why does the old man choose all the dogs?

   a. He is lonely.

   b. They are all cute.

   c. They follow him home.

   d. He feels sorry for them.

A Real Deal

Once upon a time, a little old man lived in a small cottage near the forest. Every morning he woke up and sang a merry tune as he fed his chickens and milked his cow. Then he took the milk to the village to trade for cheese, fruit, and fresh bread.

One morning, much to the man's surprise, his cow was gone! He looked for his cow in the garden and in the woods. The cow was nowhere to be found. So the little old man went to search for it.

He walked and walked until he was quite tired. Finally, he saw his cow running and playing in a big, grassy field. His cow looked so happy! But the little old man called to his cow and took her back home.

The same thing happened the next day and the next. Each morning, when he went to milk his cow, she was gone. Each morning, the little old man would walk to the big, grassy field and take his cow home. The little old man did not know what to do.

Finally, the little old man and the cow made a deal. The cow agreed to stay home until the little old man could do the milking. The little old man agreed to take the cow with him every morning. He would drop her off in the field to play while he went to the village. Then he would pick her up on his way back home. This deal made both the little old man and his cow very happy!

Go on to next page.

Directions

Answer each question about the story. Circle the letter in front of the correct answer.

1. What did the little old man do first every morning?
   a. went to the village
   b. looked for his cow
   c. fed his chickens and milked the cow
   d. brought his cow home

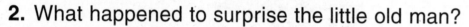

2. What happened to surprise the little old man?
   a. His cow was not there.   c. His chickens were gone.
   b. His cow had no milk.   d. The eggs were broken.

3. Where did the little old man find his cow?
   a. in the village   c. in a grassy field
   b. in the garden   d. behind the house

4. What made the little old man and his cow happy?
   a. The chickens came back.
   b. They went to the village.
   c. They made a deal.
   d. They played in the field.

5. What would probably happen if the little old man had no cow?
   a. He would not miss having a cow.
   b. He would not be able to get food in the village.
   c. He would have to go to another village.
   d. He would not have anything to do each morning.

The Silly Sisters

Once upon a time, two silly sisters lived by the shore. Every day they woke up on the floor next to their beds. They put on their pajamas and went for a swim in the sea. They ate their dinner for breakfast and their breakfast at night. They took long strolls on the beach and got lost. They spent the rest of the day finding their way back home. They planted potatoes, corn, and peas in their garden and ate the seeds that grew.

One day the sisters found a poor, hungry man sitting on the sand. They felt sorry for him. They invited him to stay for dinner. The man was happy to have a warm place to go and food to eat. But he was very surprised when he saw the sisters' strange habits.

"Why don't you plant these seeds and eat your vegetables?" asked the man. "Why do you have your breakfast at night and your dinner in the morning?" The sisters put on their clothes and lay down on the floor to sleep. The man asked, "Why do you sleep in your clothes on the floor? You have two comfortable beds in which to sleep." The sisters just shrugged their shoulders.

The next day the man thanked the sisters and went on his way. One sister said, "Now there goes one mixed-up man."

"You said it," said the other sister. "Come on, let's put on our pajamas and go for a swim."

Go on to next page.

Name_____   Date_____

Directions

Rewrite each sentence. Use a word with the same meaning from the Word List in place of the underlined words.

Word List

strange vegetables invited pajamas
habits comfortable shrugged strolls

1. The two sisters did many <u>different</u> things. _____

_____

2. They planted <u>food</u> instead of seeds. _____

_____

3. They went swimming in their <u>nightclothes.</u> _____

_____

4. The sisters got lost when they took their <u>walks.</u> _____

_____

5. They <u>asked</u> the hungry man to stay for dinner. _____

_____

6. He thought the sisters had many strange <u>ways</u>. _____

_____

7. He wondered why they did not sleep in their <u>cozy</u> beds. _____

_____

8. The sisters just <u>moved up and down</u> their shoulders. _____

_____

Jared's Wish

Once upon a time, there lived a little boy named Jared. Jared lived with his grandmother in a small cottage in the woods.

Every morning, Jared went to the well to get water. His grandmother used five buckets of water a day. There was only one bucket, so Jared had to make five trips to the well each morning.

One day while Jared was at the well, he heard a little voice. "Help me!" he heard. Jared looked into the well and saw a tiny fairy splashing in the water. Jared reached down and lifted her out of the well.

"Thank you for saving me, little boy. For that I will give you one wish."

Jared thought for a few moments. "I would like to have a bucket big enough to carry all the water my grandmother needs in one day."

With that, the fairy sprinkled some dust on the bucket, and it grew five times bigger. Jared filled the bucket. He was a strong boy, so he had no trouble carrying it back to the cottage.

Go on to next page.

Name _____   Date _____

Directions

Answer each question about the story. Circle the letter in front of the correct answer.

1. How many trips does Jared have to make to the well each day?

   a. one   **c.** five

   b. three   **d.** ten

2. Why does Jared have to make so many trips to the well?

   a. He only has one bucket.

   b. He drinks a lot of water.

   c. He wants to see the fairy.

   d. He likes the daily chore.

3. How does the fairy thank Jared?

   a. shakes hands with him

   b. gives him money

   c. gives him one wish

   d. turns him into a man

4. How does the fairy help Jared?

   a. She puts a spell on him.

   b. She makes Jared's work easier.

   c. She can fly.

   d. She likes Jared.

5. How do you think Jared's grandmother feels about the bucket?

   a. grateful

   b. sad

   c. angry

   d. tired

Two Greedy Goblins

One day two goblins were looking for trouble. Soon they came upon a family having a picnic in a meadow.

"Oh, look! A food basket!" said one goblin. "Let's grab it!"

The goblins sneaked out of the trees, snatched the basket, and ran. Shortly, they stopped and opened the basket. They saw chicken, ham, salad, cookies, and a big jug of cold milk. The goblins were thrilled. They began to divide the food. Now, goblins are not very nice. They also are not fair. Soon the two goblins were arguing about how much each of them had.

While they were fighting, a troll came along. "Look at those foolish goblins," he thought. "I will teach them a lesson!" He said to the goblins, "I think I can help you."

"Well, do it then!" said one goblin. "He has far more food than I do!"

"I do not!" said the other goblin. "You have much more than I do!"

"I will eat this ham, and you two will be even." The troll ate the ham. But the goblins said that they were still not even. So the troll ate the chicken. The goblins continued to fight. So the troll ate the salad and the cookies. Then he drank the milk. "Now you are certainly even," said the troll. "Have a good day!"

"He is right, we are even," said one goblin. "That troll was a big help."

"You fool," said the other goblin. "We are even because now we have no food, and that troll just had a wonderful meal!"

Go on to next page.

Name _____   Date _____

Directions

Read each sentence. Choose a word from the Word List that has the same meaning as the word or words in bold print. Write the word on the line.

Word List
foolish greedy divide arguing
fair certainly lesson wonderful

1. The goblins were **not willing to share**. _____

2. They tried to **split** the food. _____

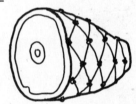

3. The goblins did not divide the food in a

   way that was **even**. _____

4. They began **fighting** about the food. _____

5. The troll wanted to teach them **a thing they would learn from**.

   _____

6. The troll **surely** made things even. _____

7. The troll had a **great** meal. _____

8. The goblins had been **silly**. _____

The Foolish Farmers

Once upon a time, a husband and wife grew tired of living in the city. They decided to pack their things and move to a farm in the country. Since neither of them had ever lived on a farm, they asked a neighbor for help. The neighbor told them, "Milk the cow and plant corn in the field."

So the wife poured some milk into a bucket and brought it to the cow in the barn. She put the bucket of milk in front of the cow. "Drink the milk!" she cried to the cow. She patted the cow and was happy that she had milked the cow.

The husband woke up very early the next day to plant corn in the field. First, he found a bushel of corn-on-the-cob in the barn. "This will do nicely," he thought as he carried the bushel to the field. Then, he dug holes in the ground in even rows. Next, he took the ears of corn and planted them in the holes. He felt very proud of the work he had done.

The husband went back to the house. "Farm life is very easy," he said to his wife.

She agreed. "Yes. We should have left the city long ago."

Go on to next page.

Directions

Answer each question about the story. Circle the letter in front of the correct answer.

1. Why do the husband and wife move to the farm?
   a. They both love the city.   **c.** A neighbor moves to a farm.
   b. They are tired of the city.   **d.** Cows are in the country.

2. The neighbor tells them to _____.
   a. milk the cow
   b. move to the farm
   c. get up early
   d. pack their things

3. The wife gives the cow _____.
   a. ears of corn
   b. milk
   c. vegetables
   d. a barn

4. What does the man plant in the field?
   a. milk
   b. leftovers
   c. seeds
   d. ears of corn

5. How do the man and woman feel about the chores they do?
   a. unhappy
   b. proud
   c. angry
   d. displeased

King Carl

There once was a mean and greedy king named Carl. He did not like to share anything. He was even mean to his family. When they sat down for their royal dinner, King Carl didn't share his food. He would eat the whole royal ham. His family would have to have their own. Sometimes he wanted theirs, too.

One day, King Carl found that he had a problem. There was a dragon living in a cave on his land. King Carl did not care for dragons. He ordered the dragon to find another cave. The dragon refused. King Carl's soldiers could not get the dragon to move. Finally, King Carl put out a royal notice. It promised whoever could solve the dragon problem whatever he or she wanted.

As you know, King Carl was mean and greedy. He was also not very smart. A girl named Rolanda had a plan. King Carl had taken Rolanda's family farm. She wanted it back. She went to the dragon and explained her plan. Then she went to the king.

"Here is my plan," she told King Carl. "The dragon will not bother you if you will agree to it. Divide your land into thirds. Give an equal amount to my family, the dragon, and Queen Carla. Then you can keep all that is left, which is what your royal highness deserves."

King Carl wanted very much to get rid of the dragon. He was not sure what thirds were, but he did not want anyone to know. He agreed to the plan. King Carl was furious when he found out what he had done! But it was too late.

Go on to next page.

Name_____   Date_____

Directions

Read each clue. Choose a word from the Word List that fits each clue. Write the words in the puzzle.

Word List

greedy   agreed   furious   refused
thirds   soldiers   royal   deserves

ACROSS:
1. three equal pieces
3. people in an army
6. went along with
8. very angry

DOWN:
2. should have
4. wanting everything
5. would not do it
7. belonging to a
   king or queen

The Earthworm

Once upon a time, a young girl lived in a small house near a little stream. She lived alone, and no one knew about her troubles.

The girl had once made beautiful clothes of cotton that she grew and spun herself. She sold the clothes, so she was able to live well. But now the cotton would not grow. The soil seemed to be worn out. No matter what the girl did, the plants did not grow. With no money for food, the girl was thin and hungry. She did not know what to do.

Then one day as she worked in her garden, she heard a tiny voice cry, "Help me! I'm stuck here on this wire, and I will surely die!" The girl looked around frantically. Finally, she found a little earthworm stuck on an old fence wire. She gently lifted the worm from the wire and set him on the ground. "Thank you so much," said the worm. "Your kindness will be rewarded."

"That's what everyone says," thought the girl. She returned to her work, and went to bed that night cold and hungry.

The next morning, the girl walked hopelessly out to her garden. But what she saw was a surprise. Her cotton plants were healthier than they had ever been. Large balls of cotton burst from every plant. She ran to the garden and dropped to her knees. Then she noticed the worms. Thousands of earthworms had turned her sick, tired soil into the richest earth she had ever seen. She knew her troubles were over. "Oh, worm," the girl said. "Thank you so much." Both the girl and the worms lived happily ever after.

Go on to next page.

Name _____ Date _____

Directions

Choose the word that best fits each sentence. Write the word in the blank.

1. The young girl lived _____.
aloud   alone   along

2. The girl grew _____ in her garden.
cotton   candy   cloth

3. She made beautiful _____ from the cotton.
clothes   colors   crayons

4. The _____ seemed to be worn out.
solid   song   soil

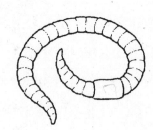

5. The girl was very _____.
homely   hasty   hungry

6. The girl saved a worm from a _____.
were   wire   while

7. The worms made the soil _____.
rich   ripe   red

8. The girl and the _____ lived happily ever after.
worn   wish   worm

Name _____   Date _____

Midnight Snack

Elena, Michael, and their mother drove to Aunt Jean's house. The children were the first to get out of the car. "Elena! Michael!" Aunt Jean called from the house. The children ran to the door and gave their aunt a big hug.

"A doe and her fawn are in the woods by the house," Aunt Jean told them. "Maybe they will come out to see you while you are here."

That afternoon, the children looked out the window for the deer. Nothing moved in the woods. It was very quiet.

"Where are the deer?" Elena wanted to know.

"They will come. I left some food and water for them," Aunt Jean told the children.

Elena could not fall asleep that night. The moon was shining very brightly into her room. When she got up to close the curtain, she saw the doe and her fawn drinking the water her aunt had left out. She ran to wake everyone up.

"Wake up! They are here," she whispered. They all were very quiet as they watched the animals in the moonlight.

Go on to next page.

Directions

Answer each question about the story. Circle the letter in front of the correct answer.

1. Whom do the children visit?

  a. Mother   **c.** Elena

  b. Aunt Jean   **d.** Michael

2. What do the children want to see?

  a. the woods   **c.** the deer

  b. a window   **d.** the moon

3. Why do the children stay inside the house?

  a. They do not want to frighten the deer.

  b. They want to look out the window.

  c. They want to go to sleep.

  d. They want to frighten the deer.

4. Why is Elena still awake?

  a. She wants to call her aunt.

  b. She wants to play outside.

  c. She is hungry.

  d. The moon is shining brightly.

5. Why do the deer come out late at night?

  a. No one is around.

  b. The woods are dark.

  c. The moon is shining brightly.

  d. The children cannot sleep.

Lucky Ducks

Every day after we moved to our new house, I stood at my window and watched an old woman walk slowly down to the pond across from our house. She carried a bag of food to give to the ducks. They always came up out of the water to greet her. Sometimes she carried a little chair to sit on. Then she could stay until the ducks ate all of the food. Sometimes one of the ducks tried to get too much from her hand. She would chase it away. The duck would turn, flick its tail, and cross the grass. It made me smile.

One pretty spring day, I poured some corn in a cup. I crossed the street to the pond. I wanted to join in the fun of feeding the ducks. I hoped that the woman would not mind if I fed the ducks, too.

It was a good thing that I went. The woman was very glad to see me. She told me that she loved to feed the ducks. But some days it was difficult for her to come to the pond. Still, she felt that she had to come even on those days. She was afraid the ducks would miss her. She told me that now that she knew I liked feeding the ducks too, she  would not have to be concerned about them. She could be certain that one of us would visit the ducks every day!

Go on to next page.

Name _____   Date _____

Directions

Choose the word that best fits each sentence. Write the word in the blank.

1. Every day I _____ at my window.

    stool   stood   ate

2. The old woman walked to the _____ every day.

    pond   woods   park

3. The ducks came up to _____ her.

    great   peck   greet

4. One day I _____ some corn in a cup.

    cooked   planted   poured

5. The woman was very _____ to see me.

    glad   gone   upset

6. Some days it was _____ for her to come to the pond.

    different   difficult   wrong

7. Now she would not be _____ about the ducks.

    cornered   careful   concerned

8. She could be _____ that someone would visit every day.

    certain   afraid   curtain

Luis and the Bluebirds

Luis walked home from school. As he came near the house where his grandma lived, he saw a very strange sight. The tree next to his grandma's house had blue leaves!

"Grandma, look at the tree!" Luis called. "Look at the blue leaves in the tree!"

"Oh, Luis, those are not leaves," she said. "Those are bluebirds sitting in the tree. They are traveling south for the winter."

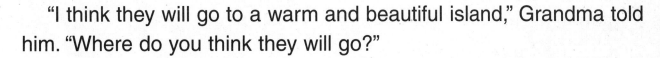

"They are so beautiful! Where are they going?" he asked his grandma.

"I think they will go to a warm and beautiful island," Grandma told him. "Where do you think they will go?"

"I think they will go to a mountaintop where there are many other beautiful birds," Luis said. "I would like to go with the bluebirds, Grandma. I would like to see new things."

"I think someday you will," Grandma said, and she smiled.

"Look, Grandma, the bluebirds are flying away. They are flying south for the winter. Good-bye, bluebirds! I will travel and see you again someday!"

Go on to next page.

Name _____   Date _____

Directions

Answer each question about the story. Circle the letter in front of the correct answer.

1. What does Luis see in the tree?

   a. green leaves   **c.** squirrels

   b. bluebirds   **d.** flowers

2. Where are the birds going?
   a. to Grandma's house

   b. to school

   c. to the city

   d. south

3. Where does Grandma think the birds will go?

   a. to a mountaintop

   b. to school

   c. to the trees

   d. to an island

4. Why do you think the bluebirds travel south for the winter?
   a. It is warm in the south.

   b. It is cold in the south.

   c. The birds do not like the tree.

   d. The birds are tired.

5. What does Luis hope to do someday?
   a. visit Grandma

   b. go traveling

   c. sit in a tree

   d. see the snow

Whale Ways

What do you know about whales? Do you know that whales are a lot like people?

Whales and people are both mammals. This means that they both have warm blood. Both whales and people also have hair on their bodies. Whales have lungs like people, not gills like fish. And whales give birth to babies, not eggs. Then the mothers nurse their babies on milk.

Whales live in the water, but they need air to breathe, just as people do. Whales can stay underwater for long periods. But they must come up for air. They breathe through their blowholes. A whale's blowhole is at the top of its head. Some whales have one blowhole, and others have two.

Like a human baby, a baby whale, or calf, likes to stay near its mother. A baby whale needs its mother's help to survive. When a baby whale is born, it needs air. Its mother helps it get to the surface of the water to breathe. It gets milk from its mother. The mother whale protects its baby.

Whales form families and stick together. Whales stay in the same family, or pod, all their lives. The whales in a pod look out for each other. They protect each other and share food.

So although people don't look much like whales, people and whales do have a lot in common!

Go on to next page.

Directions

Read these sentences about people. Look at the underlined words. Choose a word from the Word List to complete the sentences about whales. You will not use all the words.

Word List
gills   blowhole   egg   pod
mammals   calf   water   reptiles

1. People live on <u>land</u>.
   Whales live in the _____.

2. A woman gives birth to a <u>baby</u>.
   A whale gives birth to a _____.

3. A person breathes through his or her <u>nose</u>.
   A whale breathes through its _____.

4. You live with your <u>family</u>.
   Whales live in a _____.

5. People are <u>mammals</u>.
   Whales are also _____.

Draw a picture of a whale here.

A Noise in the Attic

As we sat and ate dinner, I heard a funny sound from the attic. My parents did not even notice the sound, but I heard it and so did my little sister.

"What was that?" my sister asked.

"What was what?" my mother asked her.

"I heard it, too," I said.

Then it was quiet. I think the dog heard the sound because it ran under a chair.

"Dad," I said, "I need to get something from the attic. Can you help me?" I wanted to see the attic myself. I wanted to know what made the strange noise.

"We can go up there tomorrow, son," he said, but I knew that was too late.

After dinner, I decided to go into the attic myself. As I opened the door, I heard the sound again. It sounded like feet running across the floor. The door swung open and suddenly a gray, furry ball ran down the stairs and slid across the floor. It was a squirrel.

It took a while to get the squirrel out of the house. After we watched the squirrel run across the street, my dad said to me, "I'm surprised we didn't hear the squirrel in the attic."

Go on to next page.

Directions

Answer each question about the story. Circle the letter in front of the correct answer.

1. How does the boy know there is something in the attic?
   a. He sees it.
   b. He hears a noise coming from the attic.
   c. His mother tells him.
   d. It is dark.

2. Why does the boy want to go to the attic?
   a. He wants to see the attic.
   b. His sister hears the noise.
   c. The dog runs under a chair.
   d. His father does not hear the noise.

3. Why do you think the boy goes to the attic by himself?
   a. He is not afraid.   **c.** His sister hears a noise.
   b. His mother says, "No."   **d.** He is afraid.

4. Why is the boy's dad surprised to see the squirrel?
   a. The boy sees the squirrel.
   b. His mother sees the squirrel.
   c. The boy hears the squirrel.
   d. His dad did not hear the squirrel.

5. How do you think the boy feels at the end of the story?
   a. silly
   b. proud
   c. tired
   d. sad

The Brick Birds

James watched as the birds flew in and out of an arch near his front door. The arch was made of brick. It looked as if the birds were pecking at the brick. James wondered if they found insects there. The next day, James noticed that there were small mounds on the bricks. He wondered what they could be. Soon, the birds came back and began to pack grasses into the mounds. The mounds were made of mud. Over the next week, the grasses turned into a nest. Now James knew what the birds had been doing!

There were two birds. At night, James could see the birds sleeping in the nest. They were high above his head. He worried that they could fall out, but they never did. After several weeks, James noticed something new in the nest. There were tiny baby birds up there! The mother and father birds left the babies to find food. When the parents returned with food, the babies would all open their tiny beaks wide.

James had heard of baby birds falling from their nests. He was concerned about these babies. But the babies got bigger and stronger as the days passed. Soon, the mother and father bird were encouraging their babies to fly. Once the babies learned to fly, they were not in the nest very often.

One day, the nest stayed empty. James knew that the birds were gone. He would miss them. But he was glad he got to see the bird family. Maybe they would come again next year.

Go on to next page.

Name_____ Date_____

Directions

Read each clue. Choose a word from the Word List that fits each clue. Write the words in the puzzle.

Word List
arch   often   returned   mounds
insects   noticed   concerned   encouraging

ACROSS:
3. giving courage
6. many times
7. bugs
8. small hills

DOWN:
1. came back
2. curve
4. worried
5. saw

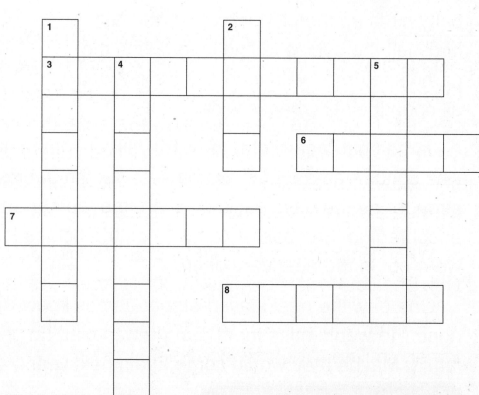

Improving Reading Comprehension 2, SV 5800-0

Emma's Horse

Emma loved all the beautiful horses. She especially loved the little white horse with the tan spots and mane. She had secretly named her Belle. Emma's father did not like to name the horses. "These horses are business, Emma, not pets," he would say. Besides, he thought she was still too young to take care of a horse. She knew she could do it. But she had to convince her father.

One morning Emma woke earlier than usual. She looked out the window. She could not see the horses. She dressed quickly and ran outside. Emma quickly discovered that the fence had been broken. All the horses had escaped! She ran back to the house to tell her father. He was on the telephone to his help. "Get over here quick," he said. "If those horses get past the river, we may never find them."

Emma's father agreed to let Emma help. They found some horses grazing just over the first hill. More horses were at the river. One horse was still missing! Emma looked across the river and gasped. There was Belle, on the other side. Emma rode up the river on one side, calling to Belle. When Emma came to a narrow spot, she rode across. Gently, she got a rope around Belle's neck. Belle allowed Emma to lead her back across the river.

When Emma's father realized what she had done, he was angry at first. She could have been hurt! But he knew she had done a fine job.

"Emma, you worked hard enough to get that horse," said her father, smiling. "You may keep her."

Go on to next page.

Directions

Rewrite each sentence. Use a word with the same meaning from the Word List in place of the underlined words.

Word List

allowed   herd   grazing   corral
convince   escaped   discovered   business

1. Emma's father said the horses were a <u>way to make money</u>.

_____

2. Emma wanted to <u>show</u> her father that she could care for a horse.

_____

3. One day the horses <u>got away</u>. _____

_____

4. The <u>fence that held the horses</u> had been broken. _____

_____

5. Some of the horses were found <u>eating grass</u>. _____

_____

6. They found all of the <u>group of horses</u> but one. _____

_____

7. Emma <u>found</u> that Belle was across the river. _____

_____

8. Belle <u>let</u> Emma lead her back across the river. _____

_____

Great Gravity

Do you know what keeps us standing on Earth? Why don't we fall off? Why does everything we drop fall to the ground? Why do things feel heavy? It is all because of gravity. Many years ago, a scientist discovered gravity. His name was Isaac Newton.

Gravity is the pull that keeps things together. The larger a thing is, the more gravity it has. That is why we stay on Earth. It has a lot of pull. It pulls all objects toward it. That is why things feel heavy. Earth is pulling on everything we lift.

The moon is not as large as Earth. That is why astronauts who go to the moon feel lighter. When they jump, they stay in the air longer. The moon does not pull them back as strongly as Earth does. The moon does pull on Earth's oceans. The gravity of the moon causes the oceans to move back and forth. This is what makes high tide and low tide.

Gravity affects all things, from little ants to the planets around us. Gravity is an amazing force!

Go on to next page.

Name_____ Date_____

Directions

Answer each question about the story. Circle the letter in front of the correct answer.

1. Who discovered gravity?
   a. Thomas Edison   **c.** Eli Whitney
   b. Isaac Newton   **d.** George Washington

2. What is gravity?
   a. the force that keeps things apart
   b. the force that makes things fly
   c. the pull that keeps things together
   d. the force that makes things move

3. Why is Earth's gravity so strong?
   a. because Earth is round
   b. because Earth is large
   c. because the moon is small
   d. because Earth has water

4. Why can astronauts jump higher on the moon?
   a. because the moon has less gravity
   b. because Earth is far away
   c. because their space suits are light
   d. because they have special boots

5. Gravity affects _____.
   a. only large things
   b. mostly small things
   c. people and ants
   d. all things

Improving Reading Comprehension 2, SV 5800-0

Doug's Dream

Doug had always wanted to be an astronaut. When he was young, he pretended to be an astronaut. He made spaceships out of boxes. He had a toy space helmet. He would talk on his imaginary radio. He talked to his people back on Earth. "I'm going to be an astronaut when I grow up," he would say.

Everyone would smile. "That's nice, Doug," they would say.

When Doug got older, he studied about astronauts. Astronauts had to do well in school. They had to study science and math. He studied hard and got good grades. Doug also knew that astronauts had to be in good shape. They had to be able to stand a lot of stress. Doug ran every day. He did exercises to make his body strong. "I'm going to be an astronaut some day," said Doug. People began to believe him.

Doug graduated from college. He got into the space training program. He worked hard. Doug completed the program. He became an astronaut. His dream had come true! Soon he would ride a shuttle into space.

Go on to next page.

Directions

Read each clue. Choose a word from the Word List that fits each clue. Write the words in the puzzle.

Word List

imaginary   helmet   exercises   stress
graduated   astronaut   shuttle   program

ACROSS:

4. finished school
6. ship for space
7. movements to make your body strong

DOWN:

1. a set of plans for future action
2. in your mind
3. person who flies into space
5. head cover
6. strain

Islands

Islands are pieces of land surrounded by water. There are thousands of islands on Earth. Some are almost never visited by people. Others hold large cities. Some islands are very warm and tropical. Others are freezing rocks.

Islands form in different ways. Some were once part of larger pieces of land. Some islands are formed by a slow buildup of sand and rock. Volcanoes form many islands. Corals can form islands, too. Corals are tiny animals that live in warm water. They have tough shells. They build up one on top of the other. They can build very large walls. These walls may become islands.

New islands are often bare rock. Over time, some of the rock breaks into tiny pieces. This makes places for seeds to grow. Birds may drop seeds. The wind can also bring seeds. Plants begin to grow. Animals also come to the island. Turtles will swim. Birds can fly. Some small animals may drift in on floating wood. People may bring animals to islands on boats. After many years, plants and animals will fill the island. The bare rock will become an island home to many living things!

Go on to next page.

Name _____   Date _____

Directions

Answer each question about the story. Circle the letter in front of the correct answer.

1. All islands _____.
  a. are frozen rocks   **c.** hold large cities
  b. are warm and tropical   **d.** are surrounded by water

2. Which of these is not a way that islands can be formed?
  a. by corals
  b. by fish
  c. by volcanoes
  d. by sand and rock

3. A coral is _____.
  a. a large rock
  b. a group of fish
  c. a tiny creature
  d. an island

4. Which of these happens first on a new island?
  a. Seeds take root in the soil.
  b. Plants grow from the seeds.
  c. Animals arrive on floating wood.
  d. Some of the rock breaks into pieces.

5. How do seeds get to a new island?
  a. They are brought by birds and wind.
  b. They come from the rock.
  c. Fish bring them.
  d. They fall from trees.

Awesome Air

Air is all around us. What is air? Air is a mixture of gases and water. We cannot see or smell air. If we can, it is because the air is mixed with other things. The water drops in air are very small. They are called water vapor. We can see water vapor when it cools. That is because it forms clouds.

Most living things need air to survive. Oxygen is one of the gases in air. We need the oxygen from the air to breathe. Even animals that live in the water need oxygen. They can get it from the water. Plants need air, too. They take in another gas from air called carbon dioxide. The plants use the carbon dioxide. Then they give off oxygen. The oxygen that plants give off is very important to us.

Air is important is many other ways. The movement of air around the earth makes our weather change. We need air to hear sounds. Sounds will not travel without air. We use air for power. Air can move a windmill. Sailboats and windsurfers need wind in their sails to move. We use air to fill the tires of our bikes and cars. The air pressure in the tires gives us a cushioned ride. These are just some of the ways that we use air. Can you think of more?

Go on to next page.

Name _____ Date _____

Directions

Read each sentence. Choose a word from the Word List that has the same meaning as the word or words in bold print. Write the word on the line.

Word List

pressure   weather   gases   carbon dioxide
power   oxygen   cushioned   water vapor

1. Air is a mixture of different **things we cannot see**.

   _____

2. We can see **water in the air** when it forms clouds.

   _____

3. We need to breathe **a gas** to live.

   _____

4. Plants use **another gas** to stay alive.

   _____

5. The movement of air makes **clouds, rain, snow, or blue skies**.

   _____

6. Air is the **force** that makes windmills and sailboats move.

   _____

7. When air is pushed into our tires, it makes **a force against the tires**. _____

8. This gives us a **soft** ride.

   _____

The Amazing Journey

Lin wished he could travel around the world. But he couldn't even go outside. He sat looking out at the rain. It made him sleepy. Suddenly, a great bird appeared in the window. "Lin," it said, "jump on my back and hold on tight. I'll take you on a wonderful journey." As Lin stepped out his window, the sun broke through the clouds. The huge bird moved its wings and they began to soar over Lin's neighborhood.

Suddenly they were flying over the Pacific Ocean. In a blink, they stopped down in Australia. Lin gazed in amazement at the kangaroos and koalas. In Asia, they grazed  the top of Mt. Everest, the highest mountain in the world. Lin reached out for a handful of snow. He held on tight as the bird swooped down toward Africa. He felt a splash as they skimmed over the Nile River. They passed low over South America. Lin saw coffee beans drying in the sun. In the Atlantic Ocean, Lin saw great whales spouting water. Before he knew it, Lin was back at his own window.

"Well, Lin," said the bird, "what did you think of the world?"

"It was wonderful!" said Lin. "Thank you so much! Now I'd better go find my mother. I have been gone such a long time!"

Lin heard his mother's voice. "Lin! Lunch is ready."

Lin lifted his head from the window sill. It was still raining. It had all been a dream! But it had seemed so real. He was glad it was lunchtime. All that traveling had made him hungry!

Go on to next page.

Directions

Answer each question about the story. Circle the letter in front of the correct answer.

1. Lin wished he could _____.
    a. fly on a bird   **c.** go to a movie
    b. have his lunch   **d.** see the world

2. What did Lin see in Australia?
    a. the Nile River
    b. the tallest mountain
    c. kangaroos and koalas
    d. coffee beans

3. What happened on Mt. Everest?
    a. Lin fell from the bird.
    b. Lin grabbed some snow.
    c. The bird broke its wing.
    d. Lin was splashed with water.

4. Lin saw whales _____.
    a. in the Pacific Ocean
    b. in the Nile River
    c. near Australia
    d. in the Atlantic Ocean

5. Lin must have _____ on the window sill.
    a. bumped his head
    b. seen a real bird
    c. fallen asleep
    d. eaten lunch

Mighty Mountains

The earth is covered with mountains of all sizes. Mountains are usually at least 1,000 feet high. Many are much taller. The highest mountain peak in the world is Mt. Everest in Asia. It is 29,028 feet high. There are also mountains under the sea. Some of these mountains have peaks that rise out of the ocean. They form islands.

The movements of the earth form mountains. The earth is made of three layers. The center of the earth is the core. It is very hot. The mantle is the next layer. It is wrapped  around the core. The core heats the mantle, so it is not solid. The crust covers the mantle. We live on the crust of the earth. It is made up of plates that move very slowly. When the plates move against each other, the crust folds. Mountains are formed. Rivers can form mountains, too. Rivers can wear away land to cause a valley to form. The land around the valley becomes a mountain.

The life on a mountain changes from the top to the bottom. The top of a mountain is windy and cold. It may be covered with snow. There is little life there. There are meadows below the snow line. Small, tough plants can grow here. Lower still is the timberline. Here the trees begin to grow. Many people and animals have found ways to live in the mountains. They are used to breathing the thin mountain air. But the plants, animals, and people of the mountains need to be tough to survive!

Go on to next page.

Name_____   Date_____

Directions

Choose a word from the Word List to match each meaning.
Write the word on the line.

Word List
formed   movements   valley
peak   rise   usually

1. come up _____

2. top _____

3. made _____

4. low land _____

5. motions_____

6. most often _____

Label the three layers of the earth.

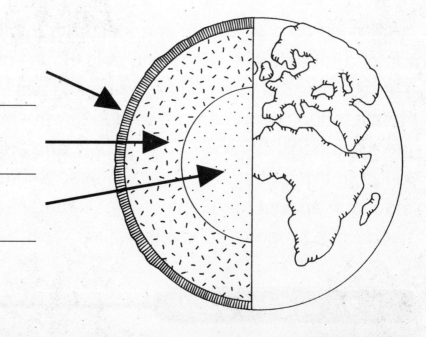

_____

_____

_____

© Steck-Vaughn Company

Unit VI: Earth and Space

Improving Reading Comprehension 2, SV 5800-0

The Planets

You probably know that Earth is a planet. There are eight other planets near Earth. All nine planets travel around the sun. Do you know what the word <u>planet</u> means? The people of long ago saw that some of the objects in the sky moved. They did not know what they were. They named them <u>planets</u>, which means wanderers.

The nine planets are all very different from each other. There are different reasons for this. One reason is their distance from the sun. Mercury is closest to the sun. It is very hot there during the day. At night, it gets very cold. Pluto is the farthest from the sun. It is sometimes covered with a layer of ice. At other times, it orbits close to the sun. Then some of the ice melts. Venus is the second planet. Earth and Mars are next. Jupiter is the largest planet. It is the fifth planet from the sun. Saturn, the sixth planet, is known for its rings. Uranus and Neptune are seventh and eighth.

Our Earth is the third planet from the sun. It is the only planet with life, as we know it. This is because of our atmosphere. The atmosphere is a blanket of air. It surrounds Earth. It keeps Earth from getting too hot or too cold. It also keeps our water on the planet. The water allows everything to grow. We could not survive without it. Because of its life, Earth is a unique planet!

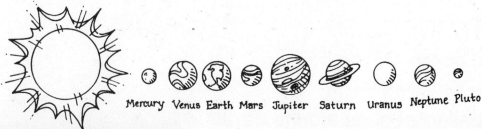

Mercury Venus Earth Mars Jupiter Saturn Uranus Neptune Pluto

Go on to next page.

Directions

Answer each question about the story. Circle the letter in front of the correct answer.

1. What does <u>planet</u> mean?
   a. round   **c.** wanderer
   b. Earth   **d.** moving

2. Which planet is closest to the sun?
   a. Earth
   b. Mercury
   c. Mars
   d. Pluto

3. Which planet has rings?
   a. Pluto
   b. Saturn
   c. Neptune
   d. Mercury

4. Why can't people live on Mercury?
   a. It is too hot and too cold.
   b. It is too far from the sun.
   c. It is too far from Earth.
   d. We can not get there.

5. What is the atmosphere?
   a. the space around the sun
   b. the water on Earth
   c. the blanket of air around Earth
   d. all the life on Earth

Improving Reading Comprehension
Grade 2
Answer Key

P. 7
1. b
2. c
3. a
4. b
5. c

P. 8
1. movements
2. core
3. crust
4. plates
5. valley

P. 9
1. b
2. c
3. a

P. 10
ACROSS
1. snatched
4. amazing
DOWN
1. sneaked
2. curious
3. warm

P. 12
1. b
2. d
3. a
4. c
5. b

P. 14
1. excited
2. baby
3. sister
4. time
5. games
6. stomach
7. special
8. beautiful

P. 16
1. d
2. b
3. a
4. b
5. c

P. 18
ACROSS
3. sparkled
4. groceries
7. bait
8. impatient
DOWN
1. reel
2. garage
5. cast
6. imagine

P. 20
1. b
2. c
3. a
4. d
5. b

P. 22
Sentences using
the following
words:
1. garbage
2. neighbors
3. completed
4. collected
5. earn
6. searched
7. extra
8. energy

P. 24
1. b
2. a
3. a
4. c
5. d

P. 26
1. c
2. b
3. a
4. d
5. a

P. 28
1. c
2. d
3. c
4. a
5. a

P. 30
ACROSS
1. canopy
3. amazing
5. fluttering
7. growth
DOWN
1. curious
2. leap
4. snatched
6. sore

P. 32
1. d
2. b
3. b
4. a
5. a

P. 34
1. c
2. b
3. d
4. a
5. c

P. 36
1. beach
2. soft
3. excited
4. terrible
5. flew
6. hurried
7. safety
8. found

P. 38
1. b
2. d
3. a
4. c
5. b

P. 40
1. b
2. d
3. c
4. a
5. d

P. 42
1. pet
2. space
3. sneeze
4. live
5. quiet
6. tank

P. 44
1. d
2. b
3. c
4. b
5. a

P. 46
ACROSS
1. realized
4. expect
6. free
7. offered
DOWN
1. roomy
2. investigate
3. scampered
4. pouch

P. 48
1. c
2. b
3. d
4. c
5. a

P. 50
1. peer
2. pattern
3. danger
4. frightened
5. aquarium
6. timid
7. treats
8. box turtle

P. 52
1. a
2. a
3. b
4. b
5. b

P. 54
1. c
2. a
3. c
4. c
5. b

P. 56
Sentences using
the following
words:
1. strange
2. vegetables
3. pajamas
4. strolls
5. invited
6. habits
7. comfortable
8. shrugged

P. 58
1. c
2. a
3. c
4. b
5. a

P. 60
1. greedy
2. divide
3. fair
4. arguing
5. lesson
6. certainly
7. wonderful
8. foolish

P. 62
1. b
2. a
3. b
4. d
5. b

P. 64
ACROSS
1. thirds
3. soldiers
6. agreed
8. furious
DOWN
2. deserves
4. greedy
5. refused
7. royal

P. 66
1. alone
2. cotton
3. clothes
4. soil
5. hungry
6. wire
7. rich
8. worm

P. 68
1. b
2. c
3. a
4. d
5. a

P. 70
1. stood
2. pond
3. greet
4. poured
5. glad
6. difficult
7. concerned
8. certain

P. 72
1. b
2. d
3. d
4. a
5. b

P. 74
1. water
2. calf
3. blowhole
4. pod
5. mammals

P. 76
1. b
2. a
3. a
4. d
5. b

P. 78
ACROSS
3. encouraging
6. often
7. insects
8. mounds
DOWN
1. returned
2. arch
4. concerned
5. noticed

P. 80
Sentences using
the following
words:
1. business
2. convince
3. escaped
4. corral
5. grazing
6. herd
7. discovered
8. allowed

P. 82
1. b
2. c
3. b
4. a
5. d

P. 84
ACROSS
4. graduated
6. shuttle
7. exercises
DOWN
1. program
2. imaginary
3. astronaut
5. helmet
6. stress

P. 86
1. d
2. b
3. c
4. d
5. a

P. 88
1. gases
2. water vapor
3. oxygen
4. carbon dioxide
5. weather
6. power
7. pressure
8. cushioned

P. 90
1. d
2. c
3. b
4. d
5. c

P. 92
1. rise
2. peak
3. formed
4. valley
5. movements
6. usually
crust, mantle, core

P. 94
1. c
2. b
3. b
4. a
5. c